Mambas

Julie Fiedler

PowerKiDS press

New York

Published in 2008 by The Rosen Publishing Group, Inc.
29 East 21st Street, New York, NY 10010

First Edition

Editor: Jennifer Way
Book Design: Julio Gil
Layout Design: Kate Laczynski
Photo Researcher: Nicole Pristash

Photo Credits: Cover, pp. 19, 21 © Wolfgang Wuster; pp. 5, 7 (main), 7 (inset), 9 (main), 9 (inset), 13 © Shutterstock.com; p. 11 © www.istockphoto.com/kevdog818; p. 15 © SuperStock, Inc.; p. 17 © Gallo Image-Anthony Bannister/Getty Images.

Library of Congress Cataloging-in-Publication Data

Fiedler, Julie.
  Mambas / Julie Fiedler. — 1st ed.
      p. cm. — (Scary snakes)
  Includes bibliographical references and index.
  ISBN-13: 978-1-4042-3838-1 (library binding)
  ISBN-10: 1-4042-3838-7 (library binding)
  1. Mambas—Juvenile literature. I. Title.
  QL666.O64F543 2008
  597.96'4—dc22
                                    2007008422

Manufactured in the United States of America

Contents

What Are Mambas?........................4

Deadly Venom..............................6

Mamba Habitats 8

Mambas in Trees..........................10

Mambas on the Hunt 12

Mamba Defenses 14

Young Mambas 16

Green Mambas 18

Black Mambas..............................20

Mambas and People......................22

Glossary......................................23

Index..24

Web Sites....................................24

What Are Mambas?

Mambas are **venomous** snakes that live in the open areas and forests of Africa. Mambas can move very fast. They can go up to 12½ miles per hour (20 km/h).

Like all animals, snakes belong to several different scientific groups called families. Mambas belong to the Elapidae family. There are three basic kinds of mambas, black mambas, green mambas, and Jameson's mambas.

Black mambas are some of the deadliest snakes in the world. They have very poisonous venom and are quick to strike, or bite. You will learn more about these venomous snakes in later chapters.

The black mamba is the largest venomous snake in Africa and one of the world's deadliest snakes.

Deadly Venom

When a snake bites, the venom passes through its hollow **fangs** into its **prey**. Many snakes have fangs in the front of their mouth, but mambas have fangs in the back of their mouth.

Mamba venom is a **neurotoxin**. Neurotoxins keep their prey's body from working. Mamba venom is very poisonous and can kill a person in about 20 minutes. Scientists study different snake venoms in order to make **antivenin**. Antivenin is a powerful medicine, or drug, that can save a person's life by stopping the effects of a venomous snake's bite.

Before scientists knew how to make antivenin, a bite from a mamba was almost always deadly. *Inset:* Mamba venom has been known to take down animals as large as lions!

Mamba Habitats

Snakes are cold blooded, which means they cannot keep their body warm on their own. They generally live in warm **climates**. Mambas live in different areas across eastern and southern Africa. They mainly live in **habitats** such as open, grassy areas called savannas or hilly, rocky areas.

Black mambas make their homes in holes or mounds made by other animals. These homes are called lairs. Some mambas, such as Jameson's mambas, live in forests in Africa. Green mambas live mainly in coastal areas.

A savanna is a warm, flat, grassy habitat. There are savannas throughout Africa that are home to mambas. *Inset:* Black mambas often make their lairs on the ground in the savanna.

Mambas in Trees

Most mambas, such as eastern and western green mambas, are arboreal. This means that they live in trees. Arboreal mambas generally do not leave the tree branches unless they are chasing prey or are warming themselves in sunny areas on the ground.

Green mambas live in many different types of trees and bushes, such as bamboo and mango trees and in forests along Africa's coasts. Black mambas live in lairs and are the only mambas that are not arboreal. However, black mambas will climb trees in order to hunt prey or to hide among the branches.

The coloring of green mambas helps them hide among the leaves in the trees in which green mambas live. Having coloring that allows an animal to mix in with its surroundings is called camouflage.

Mambas on the Hunt

Mambas hunt mostly during the day, although at times they may hunt at night. They eat mainly birds, lizards, and other small animals. Mambas bite their prey and wait for the venom to kill or **paralyze** it. Then they swallow the prey whole!

Most of the time, mambas try to get away from danger. If they cannot, they will strike to kill. When mambas strike, they aim their attack at their prey's head or chest. Without quick treatment with antivenin, a bite from a mamba is almost always deadly to people.

Because they are so venomous, mambas have few predators. Examples of animals that eat mambas are eagles, mongooses, and secretary birds, like the one shown here.

Mamba Defenses

Mambas belong to the same family as cobras. Both kinds of snakes have **defenses** that are alike. They can both spread their neck and lift about one-third of their body's length off the ground. These actions are a warning to the snake's enemies that they should move away, or they will be bitten!

Another defense of mambas is their speed. Many black mambas will move away from danger instead of toward it. If a mamba is cornered, however, it is quick to attack. Mambas are one of the few snakes that will bite more than once when they attack.

Black mambas will hiss loudly as a warning. If hissing does not scare an enemy away, the mamba will then strike.

Young Mambas

Male mambas will fight each other in order to draw female **mates** to them. After mating with a male, female mambas lay their eggs in the spring or summer. They generally lay 6 to 25 eggs at a time. Baby mambas are around 13 to 18 inches (35–45 cm) long when they are born.

As baby mambas grow, they shed their skin. The skin generally comes off in one long piece. Snakes cannot close their eyes. Instead they have a clear **protective** eye cover. When snakes shed, they also shed this eye cover. After each time a mamba sheds, its new skin stretches, or gives, to fit the growing mamba before the skin hardens.

This green mamba is hatching, or coming out of its egg. Baby snakes are called hatchlings.

Green Mambas

Green mambas are usually bright green. There are two main types of green mambas. Eastern green mambas live in the eastern part of Africa. They are one of the smallest types of mambas. They are usually 6 feet (2 m) long. Western green mambas live in rain forests in the western part of Africa. They have green scales with black edges and yellow tails.

Green mambas are **dangerous**, but they are not as poisonous as black mambas. In fact, black mambas are 10 times deadlier than green mambas.

Green mambas are shy snakes that try to escape danger and generally strike only when they cannot escape.

Black Mambas

Black mambas are some of the world's deadliest snakes and some of the most widely feared venomous snakes. Black mambas do not have black skin. They are dark brown, green, or gray. They are called black mambas because the inside of their mouth is black. When they feel **threatened**, they will hiss and open their mouth wide to scare off **predators**.

Black mambas are the second-longest venomous snakes in the world. They can grow to be 14 feet (4 m) long, but most are around 8 feet (2.4 m) long. Black mambas can weigh up to 3½ pounds (2 kg).

One bite from a black mamba can have enough venom in it to kill 20 people!

Mambas and People

Over time, people have begun to live in areas close to habitats where mambas live. This can be harmful to mambas if it destroys or limits their living areas. It can also be dangerous to people because people are more likely to get bitten by mambas if they live nearby. Although they are deadly, mambas can help people by eating rodents.

Some people keep snakes in **captivity**, such as in a zoo. Because they are so deadly, that is the safest place to see mambas up close.

Glossary

antivenin (an-tih-VEH-nun) A medicine used to treat snakebites.

captivity (kap-TIH-vih-tee) A place where animals live, such as in a home, a zoo, or an aquarium, instead of living in the wild.

climates (KLY-mits) The kind of weather certain areas have.

dangerous (DAYN-jeh-rus) Might cause hurt.

defenses (dih-FENTS-ez) Things a living thing does that help keep it safe.

fangs (FANGZ) Sharp teeth that inject venom.

habitats (HA-beh-tats) The kinds of land where an animal or a plant naturally lives.

mates (MAYTS) Male and female animals that come together to make babies.

neurotoxin (nur-oh-TOK-sen) Poisonous matter that attacks the nerves.

paralyze (PER-uh-lyz) To take away feeling or movement.

predators (PREH-duh-terz) Animals that kill other animals for food.

prey (PRAY) An animal that is hunted by another animal for food.

protective (pruh-TEKT-iv) Used to keep something safe.

threatened (THREH-tund) The possibility of being caused harm.

venomous (VEH-nuh-mis) Having a poisonous bite.

Index

A
Africa, 4, 8, 18
antivenin, 6, 12

C
climates, 8

F
fangs, 6
forests, 4, 8, 10, 18

G
green mambas, 4, 8, 10, 18

H
habitats, 8, 22

M
mates, 16
mouth, 6, 20

N
neurotoxin(s), 6

P
predators, 20
prey, 6, 10, 12

V
venom, 4, 6, 12

Web Sites

Due to the changing nature of Internet links, PowerKids Press has developed an online list of Web sites related to the subject of this book. This site is updated regularly. Please use this link to access the list:

www.powerkidslinks.com/ssn/mamba/